THE INK

Devi Dharshini

SPI PUBLICATIONS

This is a work of fiction. Names, characters, organisations, places, events, and incidents are either products of the author's imagination or are used fictitiously. Any resemblance to actual persons, living or dead, or actual events is purely coincidental. Mentions to use and connection with Indian Scriptures is completely fictional, no intentions to harm the sentiments of people were done. Author highly respects the cultural values, traditions and customs of the people and the society.

Published by **SPI Publications**, www.spipublications.in

ISBN-13: 978-81-952930-6-3
ISBN-10: 81-952930-6-3

First Edition 2025

SPI Publications

Corporate & Editorial Office
117/2, Sector 37, Khandsa Road,
Gurgaon, Haryana 122 001
Phone: +91 124 428 0743
Email: contact@spipublications.in
Website: www.spipublications.in

Processed and Printed in India

ACKNOWLEDGEMENT

By God's gift, I have a platform to put my ideas into action. I'm really grateful to spi publications for helping me publish my book because not everyone has access to such a platform.

I would love to extend my gratitude to my biggest supporters, my grandparents,Mr.Ganesan and Mrs.Ganesan...When everyone doubted my abilities , they believed in me wholeheartedly. They have always trusted me blindly and wished only the best to happen in my life . I owe them a lot for raising me, for providing a shelter above my head which always feels like a home, and for every sacrifice they made to meet my ends. I am really thankful to have them by my side always. I hope I keep making them proud!

Not just my grandparents, but also my uncle..Mr. Maheshwaran,Who is very much essential to making this happen.I am incredibly grateful for all that he has done to help me experience wonderful things in my life.

I am really grateful for all the time he stood beside me. Thanks to him for giving me the financial support to publish this book.

I want to express my sincere gratitude to Mrs. Muthulakshmi and Mr.Muniswaran, my parents for their unwavering support and unconditional love. I sincerely appreciate everything they gave up to raise me. I owe them a lot. Without them by my side, this isn't really possible.

Last but not least, I want to express my gratitude to the best people in my life—Ilakiyaa, Sri, Janani, Kirthi, Manshi, Aqsa, Devika and Sreya—for supporting me through my highs and lows. Thank you for listening to my never-ending rants, for accepting me with all of my imperfections, and for believing in me even when I was doubting myself. I'm loving you all forever, even to the moon and back.

This is for everyone struggling :

This is for everyone who is having a hard time, yet keeps getting up and trying.
those who, despite their best efforts, consistently show up.
those who prioritize their own needs even when they would prefer to ignore them.
the people who continue to breathe even when they don't want to because they have faith that the day will come when the constriction around their hearts will loosen.
This is for everyone present because they all continued to exist.
even on the days when they weren't in the mood.
the challenging, depressing, and painful days as well.

Keep going, love .

Pick yourself up:

Even on the worst days,
you have yourself only
So pick yourself up and
move a small step forward.

Remember the person who havent eaten all day,
was a person who used to follow a diet.
Remember the person who is quiet now
was a person who used to be loud and silly.

Therefore, keep in mind that occasionally,
what we consider to be the biggest mistake
we've ever committed,
may lead to even more favorable things for us.

Every week will be different;
you might revert to your old routines,
but get back up.

The best kind of love is when you pick yourself
up

Embrace your flaws :

Accepting your imperfections
is *not* about beating ourselves down.
It's about acknowledging the human
vulnerability
that lies in our innate paradox.
Your flaws will never define you,
no matter how bad you think they are,
but you will lose the essence of
who you are if you keep trying
to get rid of them.

Your physical feature,
Your gender identity,
Your deficiencies ,
Your job,
Your salary,
Your property,
Any of these won't make you
Less of a human,
It Won't affect your worth, nor
It determines your fate.

Even if none of us are flawless,
we all have worth, and we don't need to keep trying to prove it.
Any shortcomings you have are gifts from the universe.
A special favour bestowed to individuals
who shine as brightly as the sun,
high above the infinite sky, lovely and magnificent.

Let go of them…

You need to let go
They hurt you,
treated you badly With no respect.
They are just receiving from you,
and not reciprocating it back.
So why do you want them?

They want everything from you
But aren't ready to do the bare minimum.
Why do you want them close to you?

The right set of people will choose you
As deeply as you choose them.
The right people will hold you and
Shower you with all the love that you deserve.

It's hard to let go, yes i agree
But If you let go
something more aligned will find your way.
There is no loss, only gain.
Letting go isn't easy,
but it's *necessary.*

***Be kind to yourself* :**

That bad score doesn't matter,
That friend would have eventually left you,
That relationship was anyway toxic,
Those bad things that happened
are just the past.
You need not punish
Yourself for that.
You need not treat yourself
Like trash for whatever bad happened.

Don’t gaslight your emotions,
Don't sabotage yourself,
Whatever has happened is just the past.
Now move on and treat yourself with some
Kindness you deserve.
Show some love for yourself for going through
all these
Show some love for yourself for handling such
hurdles.
Just be kind to yourself.

Be your own best friend :

Your friends will ditch you,
Will talk bad about you,
Hurt you,
Body shame you,
Push you away and
At the end they will leave you.

As they leave you,
You will be left breaking
But you need to pick yourself up
And foster a bond with yourself.
Be your own best friend
No one can understand better than you
Take yourself on solo dates,
Get flowers for yourself,
Love yourself a little more on bad days

be your own best friend
Because at the end
you have only yourself
it's important that you not only cherish it,
but protect it.

Be the main character of your life :

I know what it’s like
To be the supportive character
I know what it’s like
To be lonely in a crowd
I know what it’s like
To be the therapist friend
I know what it’s like
To put to others needs first
I know what it’s like
To be the perfectionist

So it's high time you start
Accepting who you are
Who truly are.
And Own that this is *your* journey.

You are the character
the story is primarily about
the character that usually experiences the most
growth ,and who's actions drive the plot.
Be the main character of your story
And take control of the narrative.

You are enough :

You are more than enough
Even on the days feel little than that
Enough, even in the hardest moments,
This is your reminder that
you, in your skin, in your natural state,
in simply *being*—are enough

You are not a burden
You are not annoying
You are not loud
You are not silly and weird
You are not hard to love
You are not heavy to hold
Your existence is much needed in the world

You have always been valuable
just as you are right now,
so you don't need to prove it
or play a part in order to remain here.
You are more capable than you realise,
and you deserve far more than
you have convinced yourself.

You are you, you are human,
and that is enough.
"You are enough."
Let that phrase sink into your mind

Stop caring about what others think :

It's OK to be concerned
about what people think of you,
but worrying about it excessively
can leave you feeling stressed and
prevent you from being who you really are.
It doesn't matter
what you do or how you act;
some individuals will simply not like it.
It's not always about getting others to like you.

However, if you constantly feel unhappy
or concerned about what others are thinking,
try putting more of your attention on loving yourself.
Instead of focusing on what other people
might be thinking or saying,
retrain your mind to focus on what
is most crucial right now.

Finally, develop a healthy manner of

using constructive criticism and
learn to recognise unhelpful or
excessively harsh feedback.

Keep in mind that people will talk.
Sometimes they'll say something rude or cruel,
but ultimately it's up to you whether
you want to take it seriously,or
just disregard it and carry on with your life.

Accept yourself as you were designed :

You were intended to be you
in all of your true authenticity.
There has only ever been one of you
from the day of your birth to the present,
and no one else can take your position in this world.

who you truly are is who you should be
You shouldn't try to pass for someone you're not.
Or do you put on the armour and masks your ego tells you you need?
You must always act in accordance with your own nature.

Believing that we are the finest versions of ourselves implies that we accept ourselves with love, take care of ourselves, and share the best parts of who we are with everyone we come in contact with.

So let's decide to embrace ourselves as
we were formed and
to accept others for who they are.
By doing this, we stop fighting reality,
allow the seeds of peace to grow in our lives,
and create bridges of loving connection with
others.

Talk to yourself :

The practise of speaking loudly to oneself
is referred to as external self-talk.
You are not alone if you occasionally chat to
yourself.
It is a rather typical tendency,
far from being merely sporadic.

Talking to yourself may potentially have
a lot of psychological advantages,
self-talk is linked to a variety of different brain
processes, such as motivation, problem-solving,
thinking, and planning.

Although it is frequently considered
odd, peculiar, or even abnormal to
talk to oneself,
it is crucial to keep in mind that
This is actually very common.
So feel free to converse with yourself
as you navigate the grocery store aisles or
while you get ready to deliver a speech.
Don't be embarrassed to talk to yourself.

Don't rush, take it slow :

'Hurry up!' is the norm in our society.
Speed dating, fast internet, and fast food.
There is no time to spend!
We constantly have the impression that
we need to hurry or risk missing something.
We feel like we can't keep up with the pace of
life because we get the impression that
Nobody is more organised than we are.
We constantly feel either too much or too little,
too early, too late, youthful, or old.

It seems like there are unspoken deadlines
for everything we need to accomplish.
That's a lot.
The truth is that we'll grow more paralysed
the harder we try to keep up.

So, Never compare someone else's speed to your own .There are no miracle cures or quick solutions in life. Take the necessary action one tiny little thing at a time, and observe your progress.

A 1% daily improvement equates to 100% in 100 days.
There is never a time when you are too early, too late, young, elderly, or too much or too little.
Take a few deep breaths and
move through life gradually.

The little things do matter :

Prepare your preferred meal or snack,
sip some water, stretch your muscles,
take a warm bath, watch a funny or comforting movie and cuddle with a plush toy.
Do whatever it is that you find comfortable and comforting.

Give yourself a big hug and embrace.
You deserve and need that.
Even if you are unable to perceive it,
remind yourself that you are significant.

You do you . Unbeknownst to you,
the simple things you do can have a big impact on someone.
They are undoubtedly for you.
Carry on.

Self discipline is the key :

Everyone would be successful
if success could always be attained
by doing anything just once.
Truth be told, anything worthwhile
requires time, effort, and
a lot of self-discipline in between.
There is no denying the climb is difficult,
even while all your effort makes your goals
much more satisfying when you attain them.

The key to discipline lies
entirely within the mind.
Self-control demonstrates
a commitment to your objectives.
“Do What You Say You Will Do”—
whether you say it backwards or forwards
It is the same message.
self-discipline not only enables you to do tasks
but also moulds your character.

Set a goal and put the present joys
ahead of all other considerations.
Give up the good for the great,
be persistent, and have faith in your ability
to achieve your goals in the long term.
You have a strong desire to succeed and are
ambitious

There will always be a good explanation
why you can't do anything, and vice versa.
Here is where a little more self-discipline
can make the biggest difference
in your success and quality of life.

It simply requires one approach.
one action. Change one thing to proceed.
You know how to exercise greater restraint.

Discipline is the strongest form of self love.
You can do this!!

Be assertive :

you fail to get your opinions heard?
Do people readily undermine your views?
Do you have a habit of handling situations aggressively?
lack the confidence to speak up?
You may have thought at the time
that there was nothing you could do.

develop your assertiveness,
you speak up for yourself and
improve your communication skills.
Mutual regard serves as
the foundation of assertiveness,
which is a persuasive and
diplomatic communication method.

Because you're prepared to defend your rights
and speak out for your opinions,
being assertive demonstrates that
you value yourself.

Keep in mind that developing assertiveness

requires time and practice.
It will be worthwhile in the end.
You can start communicating your demands
and your feelings more clearly
by learning to be more forceful.
You might even discover that as a result,
you acquire more of what you want.

Make assertiveness a part of who you are
by beginning small and
learning how to express your desires.
You may become the person who
others think of and seek to
when they need things taken care of
with a little bit of practice and instruction.

Don't quit, maintain the persistence :

Sometimes things become hard,
Sometimes things go wrong,
Sometimes things are just overwhelming to handle,
You will gradually quit doing it,
You will lose patience,
And the need to achieve something
Wears off.

Life has these twists and turns.
Of Course we all struggle to tackle it
But you should not give up and
Keep moving forward with persistence
You will not find solutions overnight,
You need to work everyday to achieve it
Just remember that "This shall too pass"

Slowly become the person who is

tenacious overcomes many hurdles
and learns how to deal with criticism
and self-doubt.

Even if you have all the tools and drive
necessary to succeed,
you won't get very far if you lack persistence.
Therefore, starting today, aim
to be more persistent in all you do.

Persistence is going to take you far in life.

The need for self awareness :

It is incredibly challenging to modify your life consistently if you are unaware of what you are actually doing.
Without self-awareness,
attempting to create better behaviours is
akin to shooting arrows into the night.
If you don't know where the target is,
you can't expect to strike the bullseye.

You need to be self-aware before
you can achieve self-improvement,
so if you're serious about improving at something, one of the first stages is to know where you stand in clear, unambiguous terms.

We have a solid understanding of
who we are when we are self-aware.

This includes being able to recognise
and acknowledge our feelings,
even when it's challenging.
This is crucial for observing how
our actions match up with our feelings.

Keep in mind that
Self awareness can take a while.
Be forgiving.

Be responsible of your actions :

Taking accountability for your deeds
is crucial for developing enduring
connections and improving yourself,
in addition to assisting you in
taking charge of your life.
Instead of placing the blame on other people's
activities, take responsibility for the positive and
negative effects of your decisions and behaviour.

Although it is frequently a challenging decision,
taking responsibility can ultimately be
more satisfying than the alternative.
When your words and your actions are
consistent,
people will probably trust you more.
Accepting personal responsibility enables you
to assess your future actions and reduce harm
rather than blaming others for a particular
outcome .

Allow yourself to experience unpleasant feelings

when they come up, but do your best
to avoid blaming other people,
the outside environment, or
other factors that are beyond your control.

Although it is rarely simple,
accepting responsibility for your actions is
worthwhile.
The advantages of accepting responsibility
exceed the drawbacks.
There will always be outside forces that we
cannot control,mistakes will be made, and
difficult circumstances are unavoidable.
It is crucial how we handle them that matters.

Get out of your comfort zone :

Opportunities to venture outside of
one's comfort zone are abundant in life,
but seizing them can be challenging.
Perhaps you believed that there were only two options:
staying in or leaving your comfort zone.
However, there is more to this intriguing and terrifying idea than meets the eye.
It requires willpower and a shift in perspective to learn how to step outside of your comfort zone.
Each action you take to push beyond
your comfort zone results in
achievement, learning, and personal development.

Life continues to reward those who take risks, from the ancient sailors who braved storms to
discover new countries to the
modern digital entrepreneurs who have developed remote online firms.
Why?

since they were the ones who were willing to experience discomfort.
They are the ones who have accepted discomfort and the fact that life is a constantly changing, evolving, and growing process.
Because we are evolving while we are on Earth,
This process is known as "human evolution."

Why then don't you evolve?

Life feels secure when we are in our comfort zone, which is where the majority of us are.
But the development zone is where we
can become anything we desire.
You'll experience vulnerability, fear, and insecurity in that second zone,
but it's in that battle that the magic happens.
The development and learning occur there.

There is where you change.

Be more positive :

A person with a pessimistic view frequently concentrates on the aspects of their life that they dislike, which has an adverse effect on their mood, energy, and general attitude.
While some negative people vent to those who would listen, others keep to themselves and concentrate solely on their negativity.
One effect of being preoccupied with negativity is missing opportunities to experience more pleasant moments. Even pessimistic people experience happy moments, albeit not as frequently as they would want.

A positive person chooses to focus
on the positive aspects of their life,
finds delight in the little things,
and adopts the mindset that while there are many things outside of their direct control, they can select what they choose to give their attention to.Positive people have the power to change perspectives and persuade others to do the same.
They may spread positive contagions.

The majority of upbeat people are aware that life isn't ideal.
There are ups and downs,
but in order to appreciate the ups,
you must be aware of and acknowledge them.
There is generally more good than evil in life,
and you don't have to be perfect to enjoy it

It's interesting to note that
while both positive and negative behaviours
demand the same amount of energy,
they have two separate effects on your mental health:
intention and choice.
Our default state is whatever we focus on the most,and with practice, we may shift it from something negative to something great.

Fear of failure :

Fear of failure
This is undoubtedly something that
many of us have gone through at some point.
The dread of failing can paralyse us;
it can keep us from acting,
which prevents us from advancing.
But when we let fear stand in the way
of moving forward in life,
we stand to lose out on a lot of wonderful
chances.

We all define failure differently simply because
We all have different standards, ideals, and
worldviews.
For someone else, a failure can simply be a
terrific learning opportunity.
Find the source of your fear,
get through your fear of failing,
and keep going to reach your objectives.

Respect others no matter what :

Respect implies accepting someone
for who they are,
even if they are different from you
Respect enhances feelings of safety,
security, and wellbeing in your interactions.

Respect is something you can learn;
it doesn't have to come naturally.
Respect is the cornerstone of a healthy society
and a fundamental human need.

It goes beyond simple manners or etiquette.
It's something that's fundamental to being human
and required for any type of healthy interaction,
whether it be with your family, other people, or
even oneself.

Respect shields us from harm
like an intangible shield.
When we respect someone,
we don't belittle them, rob them,
or exploit them.

We don't treat people poorly
because of their differences from us.
And when someone respects us,
it makes us feel good about ourselves
and motivates us to do better.
Regardless of whether
they belong to our tribe or not,
treating everyone with respect is crucial
because *everyone deserves to feel*
safe and comfortable in their own skin.

Choose healthy friendships :

It's crucial to feel
seen, heard, and acknowledged in a friendship.
It's the most lovely sensation, in my opinion.
being able to open up to someone about your
deepest emotions, exposing yourself when you
are most vulnerable, and receiving
understanding, empathy, and confirmation
that you are not being ungrateful, whiny,
spoiled, or any of the other self-deprecating
traits
you tell yourself you are when you are in crisis.

It's incredibly lovely and true to have someone
pull you back to reality when you're busy
downplaying your difficulties.
someone who accepts you just as you are,
neither better nor worse, where you are.
only you.
That's crucial to a friendship.
The most lovely feeling, without a doubt.

Just remember
Someone who genuinely loves about you
won't ever let you give up on your objectives or your identity. They want the best for you as a person, so they won't let you be low maintenance. They recognise you are strong as an individual and want you to develop into your greatest self, so they won't let you build your entire universe around them.
They are aware that by limiting your individual power, they are limiting your ability to grow and succeed as a pair and as individuals.

There'a a Lesson in Everything, But Not Everything is a Lesson

Focus on the outcome, not the obstacle :

When we work to accomplish our objectives, We occasionally run into a number of problems. Then we turn our attention to those challenges. Therefore, it is more difficult for us to accomplish our goals when we turn our attention to constraints. Additionally, we lose focus and our flow at that time.

You must realize that obstacles are frequently encountered. You cannot reach such a goal without facing obstacles. It's possible that when you go through those, your attention will wander to the obstacles. You must maintain your composure during that period. You risk veering of course if you can't maintain your composure.

So be sure to keep your attention on your objectives rather than the challenges. You can only do it if you want to get over obstacles and get where you want to go. Additionally, it will impart many lessons that will help you in the future.

Empathize more..

One of the pillars of a strong relationship is empathy
We are better able to relate,
without response, on a human level
when we can put ourselves in another person's position and understand life from their point of view —
a circumstance, a conviction, or a difficulty.

In a way, it is a gesture of generosity—
not in the literal sense, but rather in the spirit.
We develop an attitude of openness and
teach our thoughts to be less judgmental
by leaning into this generosity and figuring out how to be more empathic.
It makes sense that empathy has a favourable effect on our interactions with both ourselves and others.

Dealing with life transitions :

A change in one's life can be expected or unexpected, beneficial or negative.
There are times when transitions occur suddenly and they can be rather dramatic. Positive or unfavourable,
life transitions compel us to leave behind the comfortable and push us to temporarily adapt to new ways of existence.
They may thrust us into a personal crisis and leave us feeling totally unprepared,leaving us feeling shocked, furious, unhappy, and distant.

However, transitional periods in your life give you the time to consider what your perfect life would entail.
You might think back on the hopes and dreams you previously had but may have forgotten about when things are chaotic.
Use this time to journal about them or discuss them with a close friend or counsellor.

Take advantage of the fork in the road right now.

Mindset is a choice:

Mindset is a choice,
so choose to believe that talent
and ability can grow—
experience better performance,
focus, and success.

You have the power to change your mindset.
The key is learning how to make the shift.
You have the power to climb mountains, brave
storms , and ride the waves!
Just take time to acknowledge, reflect, embrace
all your failures and take time to reflect and find
the purpose

In the end, the course of your life
is inevitably determined by your thinking.
A positive attitude on your boundless potential
may be able to change the current state of the
ecosystem.

Be humble :

Humility is an under-rated virtue.
sounds like a very Biblical trait.
Just because humility is outdated
doesn't imply it stops being significant.
you really can never have enough of it.

you are not always right,
you do not have all the answers.
remember what you have to be grateful for
accept yourself with all your faults
In a time when many bemoan
the world's increasing "selfishness" and "I" obsession,
perhaps we should all work to cultivate a more humble outlook.

Let yourself feel the emotions :

Recognise that you are still angry
about how you were treated,
and let that anger dissipate.
You don't have to act
as if it doesn't exist.

If you don't feel like forgiving the other person,
you don't have to pretend to.
Even after a long time has gone,
you can still feel hurt. *It's valid,*
especially if you pushed your emotions aside in the past.
Find a way to grieve, accept,and leave the pain in the past, where it belongs.
Break free from these restraints,
from your phobias. based on the past.
Life evolves.
You receive both benefits and lessons from it,
and frequently both come in the guise of very different people.
Be receptive to it right now.

This is my final gentle reminder for you :

This is a gentle reminder
to ease towards regularity rather than
drastically altering your habit all at once.
Anywhere and anytime you are ready to begin is
acceptable.
Please refrain from comparing yourself
to the highlight reel of online users.
It's never too late to work towards your
objectives, I guarantee.
Just because it's a new year/month/week/day
doesn't mean you have to change everything
drastically.
Time is a social construct, and my greatest wish
for you is that you fully appreciate the moment
at hand without dwelling on the future.
Take it slow and be patient;
you can attain whatever goals you set for
yourself.
Please take time to rest and avoid burnout.
I'm sending you my best wishes!